T0208452

A Love Letter to

M. S.

Di

authorHOUSE*

AuthorHouse™
1663 Liberty Drive
Bloomington, IN 47403
www.authorhouse.com
Phone: 1 (800) 839-8640

Published by AuthorHouse 03/11/2020

ISBN: 978-1-7283-5049-3 (sc)
ISBN: 978-1-7283-5048-6 (e)

Library of Congress Control Number: 2020904702

Print information available on the last page.

Any people depicted in stock imagery provided by Getty Images are models, and such images are being used for illustrative purposes only.
Certain stock imagery © Getty Images.

This book is printed on acid-free paper.

Contents

Chapter 1

THE JOURNEY BEGINS

Written April 14, 2019

Thanks for joining me!

Chapter 2

TO THE INVISIBLE REFUGEES

Written April 14, 2019

This book is based on my writings on my blog (Throughtfromdi.com). I decide to start the blog mainly in response to the Netflix show "Our Planet". To be honest, I stopped at Episode 2 because I simply don't have any strength left in me to finish the show. But even after I stop watching, the gut-wrenching images of animal dying keep haunting me. I need an outlet, an outlet to share my thoughts and my take on various matters because I sense something are going terribly wrong. I need to do my part to contribute to a better world, or at least, to alleviate the animal suffering. I know my voice is so small that it is negligible, but my voice and my thoughts are the only weapon I have. Use them or lose them. The choice is clear.

Growing up, I watched a lot of TV shows and movies. They made me laugh and cry, made me think and reflect, made me know right from wrong, made me who I am today. They taught me the common bond we share as human. But somehow the shows that stick with me most are not those about human interactions but documentaries about animals. their fights, their migrations, their mating, their continuation of life, are so raw, so rudimentary, and sometimes even cruel. But frame after frame, they tell us about life itself, no any other motives or plots or twists. In search of the fundamental truth about the universe, we humans either look inwardly at ourselves or look outwardly at outer space. We exclude the animals in those searches because we deem them inferior. But to me, they are equally important. They demonstrate to us the infinite possibilities of life filtering out civilization and filtering out reason. Now they are dying, because of us. They are the ultimate refugees and we can't do anything. I can't do anything either, except dedicate my blogs to them, the lovely refugees invisible to most of us.

Chapter 3

NUMBER VERSUS PEOPLE

Written April 14, 2019

A critical question in the current political debate: should the government put number first or should the government put people first? this tension between number and people is most visible in Bernie Sanders's Campaign and its critics. For example, when Bernie Sanders proposes "Medical For All" and suggests that health care should be a human right, his opponent typically reacts by asking the question: how will you pay for it? This reaction shows that it is really hard to argue against health care as a human right so the focus instead is on the number. This argument demonstrates our deep-rooted insecurity about money. I know this because I live in this kind of insecurity everyday. My worst nightmare is losing my job and can't find a new one. Because if this happens, the consequences are hunger, homelessness, loss of my dignity, and worst of all, I have to kiss my humanity goodbye. In this sense, my job IS my humanity because it provides me with steady stream of income. It translates to this mentality: my humanity depends on how much money I make. It further translates to: money first, then my humanity. So no wonder the mantra "government can't afford" works every time, like magic. Running out of money is so bad for a person, imagine how bad it will be for a government. So, this magic phrase can be used against all proposals to shore up our basic humanity needs, like health care, education, housing, ... The fiscal conservatives call these programs "entitlement programs", implying the beneficiaries of these programs are the spoiled, or worse, the theft, who steal from the riches. what's more, the economists even come up with an elegant system to explain why you should be shameful to expect the government to help you when you need help: the invisible hand makes the free market work to its maximum efficiency and allocate resource according to your worth, so you deserve what you get. If you are poor, it merely suggests you are just worth little. You shouldn't ask the government to do more because government will have to tax the riches who like you, deserve every penny they have. If you argue it is not really a fair competition, the rich and powerful have all the resources and connections the poor don't have. They will show you the math and tell you math says otherwise. BTW, never mind the numerous unrealistic assumptions in those math. In the end, everyone buys into this idea. Why not, who can argue against the invisible hand? So in the battle of people versus number, people lost, number wins. Long live the invisible hand!

Before I end this post, I want to envision an alternative world. In the alternative world, government cares about people more than it cares about number so it invests in its people to the extent that the people are secure with food, housing, and job and kids get the education they need. People are so secure that they actually want to contribute their most to the job because they want and because they can. This must be a bad society because how can it afford this. It will go bankrupt!

Chapter 4

ABOUT GOD, HUMAN, AND ALIENS

Written April 21, 2019

First, it is my strong belief that God does exist (think about the thin chance of human evolving to current state): he/she for sure will want a good future for us humans: after all, we are his or her decedents and who doesn't want a good future for their children? But other lives, including aliens (if there is) are also his/her decedent, so God should want us live peacefully with each other. How? like what he/she always does, not through Commands but through rules. In this case, it is about co-dependence equilibrium. It is simple: our lives are dependent on each other. It may be difficult for someone to imagine the aliens if more developed than we are will not eliminate us. But think about this: if we discover on a distant planet (or in your refrigerator) there is an alien civilization that is less-developed than ours, what will we do, eliminate them for no obvious gains or observe them to progress and see what we can take away from their progress? The rational choice would be latter. Then, you may ask, what if they develop more advanced technology than we do? first of all, it is not likely because we are learning from them. If the unlikely happens, they become more advanced than we do, will they just eliminate us or observe us? Well, you get the idea. Co-dependence equilibrium is the rule of the universe survival and the key to our survival to this day. If we just keep eliminating civilizations and never learned from our past behavior, the third-world war would already happen and we would already all die. As a civilization, we have evolved together to realize this co-dependence equilibrium. Why wouldn't other more evolved civilization do the same? Also, if they want to eliminate us, isn't it easier to do so when we didn't developed the advanced weapons? Just like time travel, our future self will not eliminate us like us will not eliminate our past self (one extreme case of co-dependence equilibrium). Well, mine is just a thought.

Chapter 5

THE REAL DANGER OF TRUMP AND HIS ADMINISTRATION

Written April 23, 2019

There are many vices about President Trump. Decency and President Trump are mutually exclusive subjects. However, I think the real danger about President Trump and his administration is not his indecency. The real danger is how he and his administration squander the international political capital United States has accumulated over the decades on pointless nationalist fantasies. This can create vacuum in the international sphere that leads to either an authoritarian leadership or chaos. In addition, the decline of the status of US dollar as an international currency is almost unavoidable, which will greatly weaken US's global influence further. If US can't adapt well to its decline of status (more expensive global imports, lack of talented immigrants, no well-educated domestic workers, exodus of large international corporations, hyperinflation, high unemployment and rise of extremist groups), its domestic instability will be exacerbated, and large-scale violence is unavoidable. This doomsday scenario may very well become the reality if Trump continues to serve a second term.

Blank

April 23, 2019-Feburary 14, 2020

Chapter 6

WHY WE MUST WIN THE NEW CIVIL WAR

Written February 14, 2020

This war is long over-due. Hate has been accumulated for centuries in this country and over the world. It goes by different names: Nazi, Communism, Racism, Capitalism, Free-market…Those words by themselves don't mean anything. It is the context people put into these words that's where hate resides. In Nazi, it is what Hitler represents against common sense and love. In Communism, it is what authoritarian regime represents against common sense and love. In racism, it is what white supremacy represents again common sense and love. In capitalism, it is distorted wealth distribution against common sense and love. In free market, it is sickening political interest against common sense and love. That's why we need religions: religions are love because God is love. God is not about books and books of rules, is not about men suppressing women, and certainly is not about hate. God creates this world because he/she/they love us so very much. So yes, this Civil War is no longer north against south. It is love against hate. It is God against ungodly behaviors. It is only when we win the war and rebuild the system rooted in love, we can build a world that our heroes dreamed for generations. It is only when we win the war, we can build a world that God envisioned for us when he/she/they created us. Yes, we can. and Yes, we will.

Chapter 7

WHY GOD GIVES US HATE

Written February 14, 2020

Since God is love, why we, as representatives of God have hate. That's because only from hate, we can recognize love. only from our weakness, we can recognize our strength. God gives us the self-determination, on this, we can determine our own fate. God gives us self-reliance, on this, we can build our own fate. God gives us religion, on this, we can build common bond. God gives us my family and me, on this, we can have a focal point. God gives us the property rights, on this, we can own our destiny. As simple as one two three.

Chapter 8

WHY I DECIDE TO BECOME A DEMOCRAT

Written February 14, 2020

Democrats make America Great and Democrats have a collective conscience that GOP doesn't have.

Chapter 9

WHY HOLLYWOOD IS SO IMPORTANT

Written February 14, 2020

Hollywood is my family. It represents conscience, beauty in different forms, and soft power, which is what God stands for.

Chapter 10

How Dreams Come True---Step 1

Written February 14, 2020

First, three major hypotheses to set matter straight:

1. where do we come from: God create us (cite Bible (old testament))

    1. How to test: use computer simulation to imitate from the original of life to the evolution of life, set the null hypothesis as God do not create the world, calculate the possible combinations of world formation process with random procedure, calculate the probability of our current state of living. One can reject this null hypothesis with 100% confidence. Thus we scientifically prove God do exist
    2. Conclusion: God are the Creator

2. who are we: we are created in the image of God, so we are earthly representations of God (cite Bible (old testament))

    1. How to test: all the creations in art, philosophy, science, etc in human history mimic everything in the Universe created by God. If human is not the representation, we won't have the capacity to mimic the God, we will not be given the capacity to create
    2. Conclusion: We are earthly representation of God

3. where are we going: we are going to use God as the foundation block to explore our potential (cite literature in parenting theories, Bible (old testament)

    1. How to test: we can consider and rule out other alternatives, using history as reference
    2. Conclusion: We will be offspring of God and build on God

Chapter 11

HOW DREAMS COME TRUE---STEP 2

Written February 14, 2020

How do we transit into a better world?

Once Bernie Sanders become the President, he should not focus on budget concern. Spending like crazy to initiate Universal basic income among other things (universal health care, government pay for student loans (not outright cancellation), safe nuclear energy, government paid child care, etc), then focus on every step in the chain of production on to improve productivity, meaning how to produce more and better products from natural resources. In the meantime, reform the education system, focusing on collaboration instead of competition, allowing the students see themselves as a piece in a puzzle as I suggested. Then job guarantee program. Reform the finance system. Improve science. These efforts will benefit the nation in the long-run. As long as we can ensure tomorrow, we can produce more than today, budget constraints don't exist. Like a person, if I am sure I can make more money tomorrow, I can invest more into myself today, and then this virtuous cycle can repeat itself. Like exponential equation. We should not live in a miserable state to think that in the future, we will make less and less money. Of course, on the personal level, we still have to live and spend responsibly. But as the nation and nations get richer and richer, there will be greater and greater amount of distributed income. we should live better and better lives. I approve abolish capital punishment but those commit vicious (sex, violent, etc) crimes can no longer vote or be eligible to be elected in the public office.

Chapter 12

How Dreams Come True---Step 3

Written February 14, 2020

Space adventure. science adventure. technology adventure. just adventure ourselves into the dream state. —ecstatic state.

Chapter 13

Trump Bashing Will Not Work

Written February 15, 2020

Trump is bad, really, really bad. We know this, our enemy knows this. But he still has his loyal followers who will not walk away from him. To this day, if they don't walk away from him, there is nothing we can do, or say, to change their mind. Hatred stinks but it also stays. Now, we have to make a case to people in the middle-ground why they should support us. To do this, it is not by bashing Trump, but by making our case, our vision, our future too good to say no to, yet close enough so that everyone can reach. Our task is thus to do so.

Chapter 14

LET'S HAVE A CREATIVE DIALOGUE GOING

Written February 15, 2020

Let's invite everyone who is interested in building a shared common future into the dialogue so that we can better build an enticing future no one can resist. I already started the conversation. How about using my ideas as the founding block and start building? You can like my idea, hate my idea and contribute your ideas. Then let this election be the testing ground for our common ideas.

Chapter 15

THANK YOU, MERYL'S ALL KINDS OF FANS

Written February 19, 2020

The world is fast changing and so are all facades of our lives. We grow up, finish school, interview nervously for a job (which involves preparing every little detail, reading through all the interviewing materials and tips out there, trying out all the dull business professional dresses and suits, running over numerous mock interviews with anyone who is willing to sit opposite to you), land a job, form a routine, fall in love with someone, have children, raise up children, continue the job or switch jobs, occasionally hang out with friends. Now, it also involves some Social Media shouting and profanity. Along the way, we have one facade of our lives we can count on, to deliver and to comfort. that is: Meryl Streep. Like it or not, she is there (trust me, I tried to block her on Netflix without any success). and like it or not, she is in pretty much every film ceremony and sometimes show up with very poor judgment about her dress (remember that one time she dressed like a golden curtain drape, the type that even your mom will shun away (OK, I promise this is the last time I make fun of her (don't count on my promise though))). Like it or not, you cannot move your eyes from her once she is on screen (sometimes, you get annoyed by her attention-grabbing capability). She is there, and you are there too with her. She mesmerizes you and you are willingly submerged in her. She is there in your daily life, reminding what a kind and empathetic you should behave. She makes you envision there is a better world out there, full of nice people. She is Meryl Streep. But remember, she is there because she is there for you. So thank you, Meryl Streep Fans all around the world. You and Meryl make lives worth living and worth dreaming.

Chapter 16

TO MERYL STREEP

Written February 20, 2020

Sometimes you wonder how much love is enough love for someone. What is the line that defines love and not love someone? Or what is the line the defines love and love too much? For me, I cannot discern such a line. I love Meryl Streep and this love is beyond any line. I am willing to be creepy about it and to be mocked about it. Here, I am trying to write down something that cannot possibly be written down. Simply, love you, Meryl.

Chapter 17

To Meryl Streep

Written February 21, 2020

Once upon a time, I was alone in this gigantic world full of people, and smell, and cars, and clothes, and stuff. or I thought I was alone. I didn't know there is such a thing called destiny and I certainly didn't know there is such a thing called soul mate.

My understanding is that I was born alone, growing up alone, working alone, and die alone. I am battling with this cruel, cold, and competitive world alone until the moment I die. and that's it. That's life.

Then one day, I was awakened. All of sudden, I realized, I am not alone. This beautiful actress in this small little TV box is actually a person, and she is my other half. all of sudden, the world changes color. It is no longer this dull grey dreadful color. It is full of brightness. There is beauty everywhere. The pattern of birds flying across the sky, the fading pink across the sky during the sunset, the fresh sense-awaking morning air.

Yes, During The Past 10 Years, I Have Been Acting Out, Playing A Jealous Partner To The Fullest Extent Possible (You Have To Admire My Devotion To My Role, Like It Or Not). But I Am Always Aware, You Are There. You Have My Back. You Are My Girl, My Lady, And My Soul.

You led me out of the cave, Meryl. You are my world now, once and for all.

Chapter 18

HAVE YOU EVER WONDER...?

Written February 21, 2020

Have you ever wonder: if we are just here to stay alive, why we have so many senses? Is it easier to be alive as a micro-orgasm? It consumes much less energy, occupies less space, more predictable, more adaptable, and easier to be alive. For me, I would be fine to be a micro-orgasm if there were no Meryl. In fact, I would think it is better to be micro-orgasm, for the reasons listed above.

But no, no, no, I don't want to be micro-organism because Meryl does exist. Because of Meryl, being human is so much better, much more enticing, and much more attractive. Because now I can talk to her, I can write to her, I can see her, I can feel her, I can fantasize about her.

Di

Live is no longer about just making a living. It is about the possibility of building a life together with my one and only soul mate. I can anticipate there will be bad moments between us because shit happens. But I know, I am sure that we can have a good life together.

Being whole feels so good. It conquers everything and anything in the way of our happiness.

We are one. Nothing else matters.

Chapter 19

The Capacity of Love

Written February 21, 2020

Is love innate? or is love inspired? or is love taught? In our day and age, when there is so much income disparity as there is. Has love become a privilege? Is it possible the poor cannot even fancy love or sense love or even know love? What a tragic life that is. Is it even life? or just merely retaining the capacity of breathing? I can't continue to go down this path of thinking exercise. Is this what poverty entails? OMG.

Chapter 20

"Parasite" Review

Written February 21, 2020

So the poor cannot afford love, hate, or any emotions. Even death fails them. and Dream is a luxury. Being poor forces you to be numb and forces you out of humanhood. And yet the poor exists. What a strange world it is.

Thank you, Parasite, the movie, for helping me understand this. It indeed deserves to be the Best Movie this year.

Chapter 21

ABOUT REGRET

Written February 22, 2020

I have done many things that are regrettable, including spending 12 years figuring out what I want in my life, playing around marriage to get the Green Card, messing around with other people's emotion and more importantly, my own emotion just for the sake of trying to find Meryl's replacement and to prove a pointless point that I can fall in love with someone else.

But no, I don't actually regret. Experience matters and experience is fun, even sometimes they are foolish and on the face of it, useless.

I am not a very adventurous person, but I have this uncontrollable impulse that makes me adventurous and I enjoy the ride tremendously. That's it, nothing to regret, just to live.

Chapter 22

TO OPRAH

Written February 22, 2020

You are Royalty. You are born Royalty, You Grow into your destiny. You are the vivid demonstration that you become your destiny if you work hard on it.

Chapter 23

AGE OF CONFUSION

Written February 22, 2020

In this digitized world, there seems to be two realities: one online and one offline. These two often diverge. Sometimes the online world is nicer and pinker and sometimes it is the offline world. But mostly it is online world that wins, because online world can be manipulated and sorted out and reorganized to suit one person's special needs while offline world cannot. One lives in the online world long enough will find the offline world confusing: what the heck is going on? To re-root people onto the offline world and face the dark and cold reality is one of the biggest challenges we are facing. To people in the Trump world, no, Trump's depiction about the real world and what he has achieved is not true. The economy is not due to him, the space is not due to him, the world certainly doesn't revolve around him. To people in the Anti-Trump world, yes, you are right in every way but you also have to realize there are people in the Trump world and in the middle whom you cannot simply pretend out of existence. To the people in the middle, you are probably the most confused group right now. But take a minute of your busy routine, think about if you are happy and if you want to live in a better world, then you know who to choose. See, confusion is not very difficult to sort out. Just remember, you, live, in, a, real, world.

Chapter 24

ON BEHALF OF MERYL STREEP TO THE HARVEY WEINSTEIN'S ABUSED VICTIMS

Written February 22, 2020

I can speak on her behalf because we are one.

She is sorry. She is deeply sorry. She heard about the rumors and she chose to ignore them. She can never forgive herself for this. There are many things she wish she had done: she could dig deeper and find out the truth and report the crimes Harvey has committed, she chose not; She could use her power and influence to help you to speak up, she chose not; she could welcome you and comfort you with her open arms, she chose not; she could choose action, instead she chose inaction. There are no excuses for this and she understands there is nothing she can do now to redo the crimes her ignorance facilitates her to commit. Yes, she committed crimes and she admits it. She will bear the heaviness of her crime for the rest of her life. All the glory and achievements in her career are tarnished by her crime of ignorance, permanently. And you know what tortures her more, she is known and most proud for her empathy and when you need her empathy most, she failed you. If she would exchange all the awards and praises she got in her career for a chance to prevent this from happening, she would do this without any hesitation. But the cruelty of reality is such that she cannot reverse time and there is no such chance. Remorse is going to stay with her and torture her for eternity.

She is sorry. She is deeply sorry, and she hopes for your forgiveness. Time moves forward, so all she can do now is to try her best to prevent this kind of behavior from happening again in the future and forever stay vigilant. She will donate all her fortune to help the victims in the sexual abuse and to fight to pass laws to prohibit this crime.

Again, she is sorry. She is deeply sorry. If there is anything, anything, she can do to help you, please let her know. She is here for you and she will always be here for you when you need her.

Thank you for your time to read this letter.

Chapter 25

CHURCHES SHOULDN'T BECOME THE NEW ROMAN EMPIRE

Written February 23, 2020

Suppress, suppress, suppress, suppress human, suppress human free will, suppress human free thinking. Use Jesus Christ to suppress. Us Jesus Christ as a tool. Feeding followers untrue dreams as opium. This is the today's Church. It is not the God's will. It is the church's will. And the church keeps confusing the two. Disgrace! Utter Disgrace.

Chapter 26

KRAMER VERSUS KRAMER REVIEW

Written February 24, 2020

Yeah. It took me centuries to sit down and watch this film, which was shot before I was born. With the understanding of my generation (I consider myself the millennium generation even though I was one year too old), you naturally understand why it took me so long to watch this film.

Wow, it is good. Even though it was shot "centuries" ago, it speaks to me. Yes, the package of Chocolate chip ice cream in the film is a bit of strange but the content in that package is just ageless. Chocolate chip ice cream was loved and tasted good then and it is still loved and tastes good today. So is this film. Every shot in this film is perfect, the flow (the editing) is flawless. The acting, the acting is just, for lack of a better word, genius. Especially Meryl Streep's acting. It is as good as Chocolate chip ice cream. She arouses your senses and makes you wanting for more. And the director, as if he knew this, decided to just give you four spoons and leave you in the sensation of outworldness. And her story: being trapped in the loveless marriage and the despair she felt. I feel it is me because I experienced this. The hurt and the gradual disappearance of self-esteem, I have been there too. The feeling that life is just hopeless, it is me too. Only difference is that her character took the courage to leave the marriage and I just stayed in the state of self-loathing. Kowtows to Meryl and her character.

And of course, Dustin Hoffman is smooth and other actors are very good.

It is just an ageless masterpiece.

Chapter 27

THANK GOD FOR CLINT EASTWOOD

Written February 24, 2020

Men are simple: some OK food, a couple of good old pals to play with and have a beer with, a nice car, a hobby, some jokes to make him laugh (ideally, can make others to laugh with him), a job to feed himself and his family (ideally, this job is a career), oh, yes, a family (ideally, a supportive family), and some principles he can operate around. If God ever build a operating manual for a group of people, it has to be for men.

But the world is anything but simple and is getting less and less so. and you know what makes the situation even worse, men don't like to talk, let alone explain. We already have a manual, why needs explaining. And in this world where everyone is shouting to be heard, to be understood. no one is there to understand the ones who are incapable to explain themselves. We take what is given. We swallow the sourness and we move on; we move forward. We believe action speaks louder than words. Action is the way to explain. But some simply cannot carry on anymore. They see dead ends wherever they go. They try to offer their good intention but often is misunderstood. They are forgotten. What's worse, the only time they are not forgotten, it is when they become the target, the representations of everything that is wrong with this world, in the past, in the current, probably in the future. This ever-growing gap between the men that were left behind and the charging world is presented beautifully by Clint Eastwood. His movies are his way to cope with, to explain to, and to reconcile with the world. They are also a collective essay by the men to the world. Thank God for Clint Eastwood.

Chapter 28

BRIDGES OF MADISON COUNTY HALF REVIEW

Written February 25, 2020

No, I didn't finish it. Have you ever encountered a piece of furniture that has too much ornaments on it? That's my impression about Meryl Streep in this film. She has become the chocolate chip ice cream with too much chocolate chips in it. At first, you chew on one. wow, nice surprise. Then another one, well, that's good. then another one, another one, and another one. You get confused, is it chocolate chip ice cream or chocolate chips with some cream and some ice? One hand gesture, beautiful. A little shy smile, genius. Then there is another one, another one, and another one, and, pay attention, another one, incoming. You were like, please, stop. You know what is worse, in her later films, she marches on with this "good" tradition. Except, of course, the Iron Lady, in which she is less ornamented. But of course, in most of the scenes of the Iron Lady, she plays an old lady with slow motion, so, you understand…

Clint Eastwood is good though.

But Again, I didn't finish film. I might change my mind later.

Chapter 29

SYDNEY IMPRESSION

Written February 25, 2020

The decision to visit Sydney was made in one night: a case of my impulse at working, driven by my desire to find a suitable mate. You know, the one that can replace Meryl Streep, if you follow my story. Introducing online dating magic: you can chat with someone online for about 30 minutes, feel some connection (we can both speak Chinese and English), then found out that this particular someone was in Sydney, and due to my complete lack of knowledge in geography, I agreed I would visit her in Sydney to spend New York Eve with her which was about 2 days away. next step was to find a reasonable excuse to explain to my parents why I had to be away to Sydney for the next couple of days. This excuse involved my PhD advisor, a conference, and my reluctance, and my hesitation, and my respect to my PhD advisor, and acting was inevitable (If I ever won an Oscar for acting, I knew who I should thank for). Next comes the easy part: booking the ticket, during which I accidentally found out I had to fly more than 20 hours to get to Sydney (just when you thought Google Map solved all the world's geography problem). But my determination to find a mate to replace Meryl Streep was strong and the fact that I had never visited Sydney played a minor part too. and I just couldn't waste this rare incident my parents bought into my excuse (it felt like I was handed an Oscar already). Oh, I almost forgot, I was just naturalized to be US citizen and I could not let my brand-new blue US passport down. So, I, bought, the ticket, to, Sydney.

Dreadful 20 plus hours flight later, I arrived at Sydney.

And it is a beautiful city. The airport is OK (I mean, all airports are the mirror image of each other and smelled a lot like too). Then I met my online "Meryl Streep Replacement" and well, let's just say, well, I just can't find a good way to say it except she is nice. We walked out the airport and was greeted by a warm mid-summer air. Surprise, surprise, you should have learned your geography better. She let me stay in her apartment, hosted by a lovely lady. The apartment happened to have a spare room. The apartment complex is built on a hill and we had to climb down many stairs to get to her apartment. As we climbed down the stairs, we encountered tropic trees by each stair. It is just lovely. The next day, we toured around the city. Her apartment must be located in the suburb area because there were no high-rise buildings, just cute little yellow houses in round shape. and then it was the city, I have to say at first, I found nothing special (just like the airport, all cities at first are the mirror images of each other, it is after a while you sense the unique flavor of each city). Then I noticed the sea: it was late December, the air was warm, and water was quiet, I felt calm. The next day, she went to work and I sat on the bench next to sea alone, browsing the internet on my phone, people walking pass by me, chatting, seagull walking passing by me, nodding, lovers holding hands, parents laughing with their kids, all by the light blue sea, in the mid-summer air. This is Sydney, I tell myself. All is worth it.

Of course, there is this park with tropic trees, facing the Opera house, which after you get close, you notice the color is fading. And the shopping mall, and the university, and the museums. And…. Meryl Streep, in a poster, promoting her latest movie, the Post. Well, after all, it is a globalized world. Meryl Streep is inescapable.

On the New Year Eve, I saw the fireworks lighting up the sky by the sea, in the mid-summer air of the last day of December, in Sydney.

Chapter 30

DUBAI AND THE CAPITAL CITY OF UAE, THE NAME OF WHICH I HAVE TROUBLE SPELLING

Written February 25, 2020

Just like my other journeys, the origin of this journey is "love" and determination: the determination to conquest yet another better-looking "Meryl Streep Replacement". The origin of the origin is me joining a WeChat lesbian group. Through the group chat, I identify a good candidate for my "replacement project": tall, skinny, pretty, and "rich" girl. Let's call her Wendy. I convince myself I am in love with this girl (In case you didn't notice, I am quite convinceable). Thus, the quest for "love" starts: a trip to Beijing (I need some time off from my mother), nonstop WeChat messaging confessing my "love" to her (I just get bored and want to message someone), a promise to marriage (by this time, I pretty much use marriage as a tool), and a trip to the capital city of UAE, and Dubai is a convenient tag-along (accredit Sex and City for this planning). BTW, I decide to use my wallet to demonstrate my "love" by paying for this trip (accredit all the romance novels I read for this strategy). Internet made the planning of this trip easy and the Excel Spreadsheet I made for this trip and shared with her conveniently showed both my professionalism and my thoughtfulness. I was so moved by all my efforts and she was just excited some fool will bank her trip to an exotic country. We were both happy when the trip was about to start.

The flight was not too bad. I arrived after a couple of movies. We met at the airport lobby. This was third or fourth time I saw her after we first met in Beijing. She was as tall, skinny, and pretty as the first time I met her. I was as disappointed as the the first time I met her. I was imaging an exact replica of Meryl Streep in a Chinese face. How can this be possible is not really my concern. No matter how disappointed I am, the love story must continue. Based on my abundant experience accumulated through decades of reading wide-range of romance novels, I smiled at her and faked a skipped heartbeat, hiding my inner awkwardness. We were conned into an overpriced taxi and off we go to the mirage of love.

The rest of the trip was a blur: we went as I planned based on my thoughtful Excel Spreadsheet. We ride in the Jeep up and down, up and down in the sand, we ride the camel, we eat some food, we saw moonlight dancing, and lied on the sand to watch the moon, we went to the mall, twice, oh, we also went to the mosque, the only pleasant experience in my trip(I was amazed at the delicacy of the structure and in awe of how pious the worshipers are). And we did some other things I cannot remember. I was exhausted playing a devoted lover. Now looking back, my only wish was to photoshop her out of the trip. It would be so much better without her.

On the flight back, thinking about my now empty wallet, I was full of regrets. But, however, nonetheless, based on the instructions of romance novel, my role as a devoted lover cannot end after a dreadful trip, and marriage is still in our future. The nightmare continues and continues to the point that I am completely out of gas.

You would think my "Meryl Streep replacement project" would end after this ordeal. But no, no, no, I just keep going.

The sheer determination and some vague impressions on various trips are the only precious memories I have about this replacement project, proving that if you work hard, really, really hard on something such as replacing Meryl Streep, you will be rewarded by $50,000 of debt and a full sense of defeat.

I don't know how Meryl feels about my entire ordeal. I surely hope she feels I am very cute in my pursuit of replacing her.

Chapter 31

MARRIAGE STORY MY VERSION

Written February 25, 2020

10 things I like about Bob, my "ex-husband". My mom liked him. He is economical (Cheap). He helped me with Green Card. He taught me how to use dual screen with my computer, which looks cool, but I rarely use. He likes older women, and I like older women. He is a human, and I am a human. The list just goes on and on. We don't have any kids. We planned to but the plan was interrupted by my strange manic episodes and he found it more convenient to abandon me. This counts as another reason why I like him because it is literally the best thing that happened to me, with the exception of Meryl Streep. We occasionally had sex, which was unpleasant for both of us. I cannot speak for him but for me, it felt like the express way to Hell, plus the humiliating sensation. He demonstrated to me that porn is fake and Chinese men do have big ego. He is this sad little selfish creature who is constantly complaining about

everything that happens to be in his way. He put meaning into the words "passive aggressive" and "pathetic". But he also showed me how resilient I turn out to be and it is true you can turn the world sourest lemon into lemonade if you have the right attitude. He made me appreciate life more, appreciate love more, and appreciate beauty more. He taught me what kind of person and partner I definitely don't want to be. Sorry my version of the Marriage Story doesn't have and can't have a conciliatory ending. But it is the best ending for me.

Chapter 32

Sex and Body

Written February 25, 2020

Growing up, I was baffled. I have a girl's body, and everyone addresses me as a girl, and I have large breasts and other organs a girl should have, and I have periods. But I don't think I am a girl. I mean I tried to be a girl and it just doesn't feel right. I hate every "girl" feature on my body. I remember the first time I heard that breast cancer requires surgically removing breasts, I wished I could have breast cancer. But of course, I was probably 10 or 11 and I had no clue what breast cancer is. But I like girls, other girls. They are pretty, smell good, and pretty. And I want to be a boy. I was jealous of the muscles the boys gradually developed growing up and they can like girls and say it out aloud. Then I gained this mysterious masturbation technique and every time after my masturbation, I would have some transparent glue-like discharge. I read from the sex textbook that sperms are transparent glue-like. I was so happy because I thought even though I look like a girl, I can produce sperms, which of course turned out to be false. There was only one phase I thought it might not be too bad to be a girl: the porn phase. I mean, look at the facial expression of the girls having sex. I never felt that good when masturbating. For about 15 years, I was in the state deciding whether I want or don't want to be a girl. Then I had sex. Oh, it was bad, awkwardly bad, unbelievably bad. And the oral sex, it was even worse. At first, I thought it was the experience: I was too inexperienced. Then after couple of times, no, it was consistently bad. Then I thought it was the person. After trying out couple of more guys, no, no, no, the porn is a lie. To test this hypothesis, I even paid a porn-like guy for sex with the porn-like body and porn-like penis. No, not even remotely good. And yes, porn is a lie. I decide permanently I don't want to be a girl: the only asset of being a girl for me turns out to be a lie. Oh, being a girl is hard for me. When sex and body are incompatible with each other, it is quite a struggle. But at least I learned porn sex is not real sex.

Chapter 33

My Dog and Me

Written February 25, 2020

Question:" out of the four choices, from whom you wouldn't turn away your face when you smell bad breath? your dog, your mom, your dad, Meryl" Answer: my dog. Meryl is probably a close second but if I have to choose one, it has to be my dog.

I love dogs. I wanted to say I have always loved dogs, but it was actually not the case. When I was in the first and second grade, I was afraid of dogs because they are mean, and they bite. Then I disliked dogs because they poop everywhere. But one day, I started to like dogs. I noticed their big, watery eyes, their furry, elegant body, their round misty nose and their cute little waggling tail.

I officially owned my first dog when I started college. It was a little fragile Pomeranian by the name XiongXiong, meaning a little bear. Of course, my mom was the one who did most of the work bringing up XiongXiong but when I was home, I cooked him his favorite meal: sausage with rice; I taught him shake hands and sit. He was this smart and cuddly fur ball that I was madly in love with. Until one day, he started to have nonstop diarrhea. And after numerous hospital visits, he became weaker and weaker and faded away. I was heartbroken.

One year after I graduated from college, I came to United States, my parents decided to buy another dog. This time, again Pomeranian. Yes, my mom has a thing about Pomeranian. Her name is MeiMei, meaning little sister. My memory about MeiMei was her barking sound in the background when I talked with my parents on the phone and many of her legends told to me by my mom such as how she survived a near-death experience when she was two months old and the fact that she never had any shots after she was two but never got sick.

After I graduated from my PhD program, landed a job, and bought a house, a dog is just a must-have. Entering my current dog, a he dog by the name Ruby Huang. Yes, I am the one who gave him this proud girl dog name. Secretly, this is a little revenge I had against God, who puts me, a boy, into a girl's body. I always think there is some mysterious connection between dog and God, since the two names are just the same letters in the reverse order. They also share many common characteristics in my view and I love both. But the official explanation I gave to people is that my mother's name is Ru and I just named my dog after my mom. But my mom, who doesn't know any English words except "thank you" and "I don't know English", decides she doesn't like the name Ruby so she called him Luby instead and after a while Luby was simplified into BB. So my dog's name now is BB Huang.

BB Huang is this happy little boy who likes to chase cars, the larger the better; to gossip by the window, taken from my dad; to bark at squirrels or any moving objects. He has two heart shaped fur pattern on his back which only show when he curls: one on the left and another on the right. His birthday is May 20th, which stands for "I love you" in Chinese. I consider my BB is this mysterious gift given to me by God. And he is the best gift one father can give to a son.

Chapter 34

ME AND HIGH HEELS

Written February 26, 2020

My mom likes high-heels and she looks good in them. Even since I was little, the click-click-click sound approaching means mom is coming. If I am behaving, well, I am safe. But often this sound signals danger because I am usually doing something she doesn't approve. There are many things about me my mom doesn't approve, being homosexual for one, claiming I am a man for another. But these are for later times. Let's go back to when I was little. My mom, being as rigid as a human can be, is determined to dress me as girly as possible. Skirts, dresses, are her favorite decorations for me. Naturally, I hate them. I like pants with a lot of pockets. But somehow, we always manage to reconcile our differences in the dress codes. But there is one dress code the two of us failed to reach consensus: the high heels. Before I came to United States, high heels were not on her priority list.

Then, when I returned to China in one summer, my mom decided it is time. It is time for me to shine in all the glory of high heels. That's when all the fun starts. She took me to the mall, helped me to choose two or three pairs of high heels. She was careful with her ambition: she started with low wedged high heels to warm me up. I tried in the mall. It was not too bad. My feet hurt a little and my walking was uncomfortable, but I can manage, in the mall, with smooth floor and everything. I gained confidence: I can look at pretty as my mom (remember I was still in the porn phase). But the minute I walked out the mall and stepped on the cemented sidewalk, the pain just rushed in. It is like all the physics class rolled in in one second: you learned everything about slope, pressure, friction, action and reaction. No, you don't need all the math, your senses will teach you. But being a strong and confident "woman" like my mom, I started walk, experiencing physics class on every step. As it turns out, I was not as strong and confident as I had hoped, I gave up the wedged little high heel the next morning, resorting to the comfort of my sneakers. You think my mom would take the cue and gradually forgot about her little ambition. But no, you are dealing with a very strong-willed woman who loves high heels very much. Her strategy was forcing me to practice. The case she presented was that as I walk more in high heels, my feet skin would get thicker, which would numb the pain. She then showed me the thick feet skin she developed. Growing up worshiping my mom, I was convinced. Case closed. I started to practice. Or put it in my mom's words, I started to thicken my feet skin, bearing all the pain, in hope of making my mom happy. My mom even sent her assistant: my dad, as my sidekick in this practice.

We would walk together to get my mom from work so that I can practice. I remember once I complained to my dad that high heels are the worst invention to torture women (I am always more of myself with my dad). My dad would hear my complain and encouraged me to take another small step: one small step in high-heels, one giant step towards my womenhood. When we walked back home together, my feet would bleed like I was back from the battlefield. That's when band-aid came in handy. My mom would be proud of me: these scars borne witness of my growth into a strong and confident woman as she is and as she has hoped for me to be. This practice continued for couple of days. Eventually, my parents love for me won and high heels were forever left in the shoe box. But my mom never completely loses her hope for me in high heels. She continues to buy me high heels in various forms and shapes. I, being an experienced mom-handler, would try these shoes for one day or one half-day, and never wear them again. But my mom surely looked good in her high-heels and the click-click-click sound becomes part of my fond childhood memory about my lovely mother.

Chapter 35

One Child Nation (My Experience)

Written February 26, 2020

I was born a girl, growing up in a girl's body. I was a happy kid surrounded by love: my parents are devoted to me; my granddad on my dad's side loves me because out of his four grandkids, I am the only girl; my grandmother on my mom's side loves me because my granddad on my dad side used to be her superior in the army and according to her, saved her life once by removing her from a truck later had a fatal accident, and she was the matchmaker in my mom and dad's marriage; most of my aunts and uncles love me; my neighbor adores me because I was a pretty cute kid. I would wonder around my grandparents' (on my mom's side) apartment complex which felt like a garden to me, carrying a fake gun on my back, on various rescue missions with no idea what to rescue, and these missions usually end up with me in the treasure land, the grocery store, licking the cap of this huge soy bean bucket, the smell of which was so tempting. It was a good summer. I would occasionally play with my neighbor's kids but not too much: I was too clumsy to play with the girls and I ran not fast enough to play with the boys. My only competition at home was from my cousins, or this particular cousin, who was sent to also live with my grandparents. She would steal my grandparents' attention and I hated her, so I bullied her when my grandparents were not around because I am one year old than she is and I was much taller (according to the legend, I was born very long). Later on, we both sensed there was actually no competition: my grandmom liked me more while my granddad liked her more, so we share. I was aware of such thing as brothers and sisters, but I thought my cousins are my brothers and sisters. This thought continued to my middle school, I got to know this girl who has an older sister in real life. Wow, that opened a door for me. I started to wonder how I would feel if I had a brother or sister. First of all, I wouldn't want to be the oldest because oldest would mean more sharing with the younger ones. Ideally, I would want an older brother because it would appear cool and he would protect me and based on how good looking I am, he would be a very handsome big brother. Sisters, older or younger, are not so such of my desire: I had enough with my cousin and sisters are too girly. Of course, I was fully aware that I could only have younger brother or sister now even if I beg my parents for a sibling. So no, I am happy the way I am. But I still wish for an older handsome protective brother. I shared the story about the girl who has a sister with my parents and their reaction was how could they? It was against the law. I gained this awareness that her parents broke the law and she was immediately downgraded from cool kid to uncool kid and stay on my uncool kid list for the rest of my middle school. From this point onward, I started to hear more about China's one child policy and some horror stories about my distant relative in the rural area in ShanXi province sent their daughters in hiding so they could have a son. I even interacted with one of such daughters. Throughout my interaction with her, I always keep this awareness that she was this unwanted daughter. I since have mixed feelings about families which have multiple children: they broke the law, it is unfair, but it is nice they have a large family. Then I came to United States, I was more fully aware of China's one child policy than I was in China. I remember in one incident, I ran into this middle-aged guy, once he learned I was from China, his reaction was how lucky I am that I am still alive, and I am able to come to United States. I knew what he meant because I heard about these horror stories. At the same time, I wanted to tell him I am not a lucky kid, I am just a normal kid who had a normal childhood and was very much loved and cared for. Then in the first couple of years after this incident, whenever I ran into a middle-age or an old white stranger, I was on full alert: I didn't know how to explain my story, my country's story, and how these two differ. Then after a while, this fear subsides, and I gained ownership of my own story and I don't give a damn about how these white people think of me. My story goes like this: I grew up a happy kid. I got everything I ever needed and even more. But I am fully aware of what happened under China's one child policy and other terrible things happened to various group of people fighting for human rights. These are the sins of this country, not mine. I fought hard to come to United States to escape my doomed and hopeless future in China. I, as an individual, am entitled to my own happiness. And I, as people, will fight as hard as I can to my capacity for the happiness of the others.

Chapter 36

MY COLLEGE LOVE AFFAIR

Written February 26, 2020

There was nothing much to be said about my college years in my hometown: Chengdu. These are four dull years. The only bright color in my life is this pretty girl. She is so pretty that she is considered by many as the College Flower, a rather communist name for the Prom Queen of a sort. Our friendship starts with a plot: I heard about this amazing beauty from my close high school friend who went to the same college as I am and I am pretty sure she is also gay. She was an average student in my high school while I was, based on my own criteria, a rock star. My English grades were consistently great, I was good looking as always, my math was good, I was cool (and of course I still am), and I directed a school play. To be more exact, I sort of produced that play by choosing the script and putting together an ensemble of the director, cast, and administrative staff. Well, she was one of my staff. You know our comparative status in my view. And I finished my rock star status with a high note: I got a pretty high score in the National College Entrance Exam.

Then, it all comes to an abrupt end: I had a bone tumor on my leg and had to postpone my entrance to the college by about a month, which completely ruined the grand opening of my college year I planned for myself since well, my College Entrance Exam score about about 50 points higher than the admission score of the College. It is a pretty big deal since the highest score you can get is a little over 600 points. I deserve to get to continue my rock star status and be treated accordingly. The tumor ruined everything. What's worse, I had to walk around the campus on crutches and bring a nanny with me everywhere I go on campus. I felt doomed. Then entering my high school friend, who barely passes the admission score but arrives at the campus on time without any delay, so she is well adapted to the college life already by the time I arrive at the campus, with crutches and a nanny. When I heard about this College Flower during lunch with my friend, I see hope. I can regain my rock star status by befriending this College Flower and ideally by making her fall in love with me. I conquer the College Flower; thus, I conquer the College. I started the plot to befriend this College Flower, who is in the same major and same year as I am, and her dorm is on the same floor as mine. And her dorm mate is good friend of my dorm mate. I see opportunity. I first befriend her dorm mate when she visits her friend, my dorm mate, in our dorm. Then I visit her dorm many times and of course, often bump into the College Flower, who naturally become my friend since we are both Chengduese and we happen to share a lot of things in common. The only inconvenience is one of our commonalities is the love for romance and when I met her, she was hopelessly in love with a good-looking tall guy who happened to pass by her in a garden. Of course, she has no idea who that guy was, which school he was in, or which year he was in. Basically, besides the fact that he was good-looking and tall and handsome, she knows nothing about him. She has her own plot: she would wait in the garden and "accidentally" run into this guy and make him fall in love with her. As you can see, the conflicts of our plots emerge. Me, being me, a problem solver, come up with some twists of my own plot to accommodate her plot: I would wait with her in the garden and then make her fall in love with me. The timing is crucial, I have to make her fall in love with me before she makes the faceless good-looking guy fall in love with her. Oh, I tried my charm while we wait in the garden, the details of which I don't remember. All I know is that we never ran into that good-looking guy in the garden and to this day, I still don't know whether my charm worked or not because I am not so sure whether she fell in love with me or not. Yes, during the four years in College, I spend all my efforts and time to conquer her so that I can conquer College and conveniently forgot the original functionality of College. I floundered pretty much all of my college classes and had to take two make-up exams. Along the way, I discovered that I am actually pretty smart because I can cram an entire semester worth of schoolwork into my brain in one or two nights of study and manage to pass. I am still proud of my such feat to this day. As to my plot and the College Flower, at the end of the fourth year, I made this convincing argument to myself: It is best for me not to know whether she is in love with me or not, because if she is (which I highly doubt), I would not know how to continue our love affair because life is hard for lesbians and being a high-quality lover, I would not want her to go through this ordeal; and if she is not (which is highly probable), that means I wasted my entire four years in College and it is a sour defeat to swallow. However, my College life cannot end in this big unknown. I manage to fall in love with another girl, confess, get rejected. After several bottles of hard liquor, some tears, and some mourning, and a poem if I remember correctly, case closed.

After graduating from College, I took a brief internship in a small company, and being a good-looking romantic guy as I am (btw, I shed a couple of pounds after my sad fourth year in College), I think I attracted my lady boss and of course, I have to reciprocate given what I went through in College. That couple of months of my imaginary love affair with my lady boss were intense. I secretly vowed to myself to love her to death and rescue her from her loveless marriage (yes, she was married, and her husband was actually quite nice). I would get the highest paying job in the world and we would live happily ever after. United States, being the richest country in the world, is the place where the highest paying job is located, so it is my destination. This works nicely to my original plan ever since middle-school to come to United States. You see, I always have a way to work plans into plans into plans. One thing I forgot to mention is that during my busy sad fourth year in College, I half-hearted studied TOFEL and GMAT and applied to a random school and applied for a visa and got rejected as expected. So my love affair with my boss lady gave me motivation to work harder on my visa application to get to United States, to study hard, to work hard, and to land the highest-paying job in the world, and then victoriously come back to get my girl, the boss lady, who is about 15 years senior than I am and was probably happily married. How the boss lady thought about my plan? I was too shy to ask and considered as of little relevance. Driven by my new-found love and courage, I applied for another random school, with the help of an agency, which helped my personal statement and other sorts of things that studying abroad needed. Looking back, I notice how lazy I was back then to not even bother to write a good personal statement, which I was fully capable of. The part I worked hardest on was to get my transcript right. Given my above-mentioned study record in my college, I had to do some window dressing to match the 3.0 GPA threshold. Luckily, my mom knows someone who knows someone who knows someone who can remove some of the bad grades I had. It was quite an effort to raise my GPA to 3.0. Yes, I was that bad. I didn't conquer college at all, as it turns out. I applied for US visa and got rejected about 6 times in that year and at the 7th time, I pass. I hurried to fly to United States because by that time, the semester has already started.

Chapter 37

MY YEAR IN BRIDGEPORT

Written February 26, 2020

To prepare for my stay in United States, my mom is determined to make me as comfy as I can be in US by packing everything, she can think of in the two suitcases. She has never been to United States. Even though she is fully aware that US is a highly developed country, she is determined to set her expectation about US as low as possible. Everything means everything. Back then, the airline companies haven't set the size limit on the suitcase. My mom seizes this loophole and bought two largest suitcases I think man ever made from I don't know where. I never saw suitcase that large then and I have never seen suitcase that large ever since. Carrying two largest suitcases with everything my mom prepared for me, I arrived at the random school my agency applied for me. It takes me a few days to remember the name of the random school: University of Bridgeport. It takes me even longer to remember the state: Connecticut. It takes me another 7 or 8 years to pronounce Connecticut correctly.

University of Bridgeport is a University for sure. But it is not quite what I had expected. It is not cool: the campus is small, and the buildings are old, and the town is a broken town. It makes me realize there is a long way to go from here to the highest-paying job I have planned for me and my boss lady. I decide to study hard. But before I can study, I have to take care of some inconveniences: first, it is the all the administrative things I have to take care of such as registration and some medical stuff, then it is the friends stuff, as it turns out, the agency I used sends out an army of previously successful cases to search for me to make sure I am safe. Naturally, we all become friends. Then it is the dorm, I get assigned to a dorm with another newly arrived Chinese girl whose dad is in coal mining business, which means she is probably very rich, but I didn't know back then. We were friends initially because everything is fresh, and I feel like to use my charm to make as many friends as possible. The minute we move into the dorm together, I start to find her annoying. First, it is her accent. It is not her accent per se. it is the fact she talks on the phone nonstop with her parents that makes her accent unbearable. Second, she seems to be in a hurry a lot and I like to do things slowly. Third, and most importantly, it is the masturbation situation. I occasionally lived in my dorm in my college years because the school took attendance, but we had tent on each bed so I could masturbate under the tent. But now, in this new dorm, there is no tent! that means I have to wait for her to fall asleep if I want to masturbate. That's just annoying. The dislike is mutual. We start to bicker a lot.

Luckily, the RA intervenes, and more luckily, the University is not very popular, and it has some spare empty dorms. I get assigned to an empty dorm without extra charges. I regain the freedom to masturbate whenever I want. Yeah!

Now all that non-study-related stuff has been taken care of, I can focus on my study. But not yet, there is one more thing: an uncle my mom introduces me to who is supposed to look after me. This uncle was my mom's friend's friend. He and my mom found each other mutually useful. He can help me and actually tried to help me to apply for US school and to get to US. My mom can help him with his affairs in China. This uncle has something else in mind for me: he finds me a nice fit for his still single nephew and someone who can be handy to help his business. he rushes me to finish my school quickly. He even sets up a date between me and his nerdy nephew, and… his nephew's mother. My mom also has high hope for this date. Needless to say, the date is doomed from the beginning given my plan for me and my boss lady. But I like my mom and don't want to disappoint her. I dress up nicely the morning of this doomed date. However, thirty or some minutes before the nerdy nephew and his mom's arrival, I had a huge fight with my dorm mate and didn't have time to look at mirror and notice there is a large blue ink stain on the chest of my nice white shirt. And during the entire date day, I didn't have time to look at the mirror. It is until that evening I notice this stain, but it doesn't matter anyway, I have already decided I dislike the nerd and his frowning mother. This date, combined with our difference in opinions about my future, I start to ignore phone calls from the uncle until he completely fades away in my life.

That's when the study starts and it is fun, rewarding, and refreshing. I discover that English and knowledge are a perfect match. The knowledge flows in English and the concepts I struggled a lot in college all make sense now. The professors are reasonably good, compared to my college professors anyway. I particularly like my Statistics professor, a nice Korean grandpa who speaks perfect English and explains the concepts intuitively. The textbooks, the textbooks, are written in a plain language I can understand, unlike the Chinese textbooks, which felt like written in a coded language. I regain confidence in myself and in knowledge. I just want to study. Of course, I didn't forget my boss lady and my plan for us.

All plans aside, I was secretly in love again, with a Malaysian Chinese girl who lives on the same dorm floor. We often run into each other in the bathroom. She is much cooler than my Chinese friends because she is American, and her English is much better, and my Chinese friends are constantly fighting with each other. We started to go to the dining hall together. She will drive me back and forth in her car. Oh, I almost forgot, she has a car while none of my Chinese friends have a car (considering we all just arrived in US, it shouldn't surprise anyone). and her body is nice too. I cannot help but fall in love with her. What else can you do to show your appreciation? Learning from my past lesson, I decide to not to bottle up my feelings. I write her a note every day and slip it underneath her door and after a while, she senses my love and I confess, and then here I am, in the consulting office because she files a complain that I harassed her. Ok, end of the story. Let's go back to my boss lady.

It was in my year in Bridgeport, I first met and befriended a gay friend. He was among the army of agency success stories who went out looking for me. I remember we were from the same province and I felt this instant connection with him because he dresses very properly. He is the type of gay you can sense without a gaydar. He is practically screaming I am gay. I easily get out a confession from him and I confess to him too. He is warm, kind, sassy, and girly. I was surprised to learn he is the man role in the relationship. I heard about all the colorful stories from him about gay sex and it is my first time. We also reached a consensus that all men are born gay, or at least 3 quarters of them are gay. Needless to say, I found my new masturbation material: gay sex. We both agree that Bridgeport should not be our final destination and we should transfer, and we give each other tips about preparing transferring material. He transferred one semester earlier than I do to University of Buffalo and I transferred to University of Connecticut. I chose UCONN because of its location. My friendship with him was a strange sensation: you finally found your kind, you are not lonely anymore, it feels warm and fuzzy, and yet, it is annoying. It is annoying because he is constantly complaining. He will get upset about one tiny wrinkle on his shirt, or about the food, or about the weather. He constantly updates you on his relationship status and every little detail about his breakups and makeups. He shares skin-care tips with you which you just don't care. After he transferred, we keep contact. Gradually, he faded away from my life too. But he is one rare individual who I often think of and think of fondly.

Chapter 38

In UCONN

Written February 26, 2020

Bridgeport, just as the name indicates, serves as the bridge between China and US for me. It took me one year to across the bridge and here I am, in the graduate dorm of University of Connecticut. By the time I arrived at UCONN in the summer, I already bought a car, a brand-new Mazda. I can choose between living in the dorm and renting an apartment. I chose the dorm because of its proximity to School of Business and I just want a place to study. I really don't care about where I live. The graduate dorm of UCONN is a perfect fit for me because anyone who cares about their living condition will not choose this dorm. In the year in Bridgeport, I experienced everything from love to friendship, and now I am determined to concentrate on studying because it feels really good and it feels right.

I was accepted into UCONN MBA program, which is the only choice for me in business. Back then, MBA was at its peak and it was the only thing a lot of Business Schools offered besides accounting. Conveniently for UCONN and for me, UCONN's accounting program is online and me, as an international student, can't maintain my visa studying online program, leaving me with no choice. I like this situation because I find choosing is very time-consuming and effort-consuming and usually involves a great deal of headaches. To prepare for MBA program, I enrolled in UCONN summer school to take some accounting classes. Just as I expected, I enjoyed my classes tremendously. I don't care about where I sleep, where I eat, or what I eat, I just want to learn. This smoothness continues to the beginning of my MBA program and stops there. As I learned the hard way, MBA program is not for learners. I struggled great deal in the program and learned practically nothing because everything presented to me is in piecemeal and I don't see any connection in between classes whatsoever. Me, being me, never accepting defeat. I start to shop around for a better way and more coherent way to learn. I considered CPA program but decided against it because it will not land me the top-paying job I had in mind for me and the boss lady. I then considered finance. I decided it is the best choice for me for several reasons: one, I can work hard to land a job in Wall Street. It is the top-paying job I had in mind. Two, I can combine my MBA study with my finance study seamlessly. Three, I really want to understand Wall Street Journal. I think the Journal looks pretty cool and many important people read it every day. I found out there is a certification program for finance too, just like CPA, called CFA. I googled CFA and decided this is the certification I would pursue so that I can learn. The decision about CFA turns out to be one of the best decisions I ever made: I indeed learned a lot about finance and in a systematic and coherent way as I had hoped. I stumbled through my MBA program and spend most of my time and effort on studying CFA curriculum. I was in heaven. yes, the material is a little bit challenging, but I like that and I am learning something fascinating. More importantly, I learned how to learn on my own. and I am non stoppable from there. Yes, I took some classes here and there in my second masters and Phd program but learning on my own makes everything I learn into one coherent system and I see the world in a different light, and I see God. The minor setbacks that I never landed a job on Wall Street and my plan about me and the boss lady never worked out mean nothing to me now. I am just happy.

Along my journey, I met many interesting and fun people from all colors and races and nationalities. They are my friends, my professors, my advisors. Their humanity is essential for me to see God. and to know God see us.

And I am determined to make this world a better place because I see no alternatives.

Chapter 39

IN THE PURSUIT OF HAPPINESS

Written February 27, 2020

Looking back, I have always been in search for something, something at the time I couldn't describe, imagine, or envision. It is happiness. I always thought I was happy growing up because I felt light. I can skillfully abandon anything that felt heavy to me and move on. But lightness is not happiness. For me, happiness is Meryl Streep, to be able to reunite with her again, to feel whole again, to sense the uncontrollable heart beats again, to see her smiley face again, and to have a real conversation with her again, and to hear her giggle again. My aimless wondering ever since childhood has been aiming at her.

Looking back, the first time I fell in love was due to the smell of the girl's hair, and that reminds me of how Meryl's hair smelled like. I soon learned how to masturbate. I wanted to be a boy because I was afraid being a girl would disappoint her. My second love was a girl who looked a little like her especially when she smiled. High school, I felt attracted to a boy who I thought she would like, and I wish I could look like him. My college love looks like her too. I felt for a girl for touching hand because that sensation reminds me of her. The boss lady at the company I worked has giggles and voice like her when she was young. The drive to come to United States after 8 rejections was to find her since somehow, I knew she is in US. After I came to US, I felt for any girl who bears slightest resemblance to her. I was so happy when the first time I realized it was her during my first manic episode in the car. Then it was utter disappointment when I lost hope to find her. That's when I submit to my mom's persuasion to get married. I married a random guy who can give me green card. Then it is the mission to find her replacements, which results in disappointments time and time again.

Looking back, my whole life is about her, Meryl. It is unbelievable but it is true. That concludes my first 40 years. It is not about the quest for knowledge even though I am curious. It is not about saving humanity even though I care about humanity. It is not about proving God exists even though it is nice to have it proven. It has been, and will always be, to find my eternal love, Meryl, now and in the future. This is my destiny. This is my pursuit for happiness.

Chapter 40

A Love Letter to God

Written February 27, 2020

Dear God,

Thank you for giving birth to me and Meryl and creating a beautiful and magnificent world. Every day, I am stunned by the world's beauty. Every day, I am in awe of your creation. I used to think you create the world so that one day, we can give something back to you. But my experience with Meryl taught me that not everything is transactional. You don't expect anything in return if you truly love someone. You just want to give and give and give, give everything you have and one smile from the one you love is rewarding enough. That must be why you give birth to us. And you respect us totally, including our free will to determine our destiny and rely on ourselves. You give us a home, the earth, and you give us the expansive universe to explore. You are simply the best parents.

Di

I don't know how heartbroken you are seeing us on this self-destruction path.

All I can do is to get my writings published and tell the world who I am and what I have experienced and endure what comes next.

This is my love letter to you, my God. For you, I am willing to be crucified again. For you, a thousand times.

About the Author

Who am I? Where I am from? Where I am going? The old me would say: it is not important, it doesn't matter, it is none of my business. What would I answer now? Read this book, if you understand, you understand; if you don't understand, my old answers still apply.

Printed in the United States
By Bookmasters